JB
Damien

Brown, Pam

Father Damien

FATHER DAMIEN

by Pam Brown

Picture Credits

Bob Abraham — 14, 25, 28, 40, 51, 57; APA Photo Agency, Singapore — 29 (both), 44; Mary Evans Picture Library — 8 (top), 34, 35; Hawaiian Tourist Board — 4, 6, 13, 17, 21, 22, 32 (both), 56; Leprosy Mission — 59, 60, 61, 62 (top), 63 (both), 64; LEPRA — 58; The Picpus Fathers, Louvain — 11, 18, 31, 37, 42, 43, 47, 53, 55; Ann Ronan Picture Library: 8 (bottom), 9; United Society for the Propagation of the Faith — 26 (both), 27, 62. We have been unable to trace the copyright holder of the pictures on page 7 and would welcome any information that would enable us to do so. Maps drawn by Geoffrey Pleasance.

Our special thanks go the Picpus Fathers in Louvain for their support and for supplying the pictures, without which this book would not have been possible. The Damiaanmuseum in Tremeloo has many items connected with Damien and his life.

To Emily

North American edition first published in 1988 by
Gareth Stevens, Inc.
7317 W. Green Tree Road
Milwaukee, WI 53223 USA

Library of Congress Cataloging-in-Publication Data

Brown, Pam, 1928-
    Father Damien: the man who lived and died for the victims of leprosy.
    (People who have helped the world)
    Includes index.
    Summary: Presents a biography of the priest who gave his life to the care of lepers in a colony at Molokai, Hawaii.
    1. Damien, Father, 1840-1889 — Juvenile literature. 2. Catholic Church — Clergy — Biography — Juvenile literature. 3. Misisonaries — Hawaii — Biography — Juvenile literature. 4. Missionaries — Belgium — Biography — Juvenile literature. 5. Missions to lepers — Hawaii — Juvenile literature. [1. Damien, Father, 1840-1889. 2. Missionaries] I. Title. II. Series.
BX4705.D25B76 1988 266'.2'0924 [B] [92] 88-2106
ISBN 1-55532-815-6 (lib. bdg.)
ISBN 1-55532-840-7

Series conceived and edited by Helen Exley.
Picture research: Diana Briscoe.
Research assistant: Margaret Montgomery.
Series editor, U.S.: Rhoda Irene Sherwood.
Editorial assistant, U.S.: Mary Thomas
Additional end matter, U.S.: Ric Hawthorne.

Printed in Hungary

1 2 3 4 5 6 7 8 9 93 92 91 90 89 88

FATHER DAMIEN

The man who lived and died for the victims of leprosy

by Pam Brown

Gareth Stevens Publishing
Milwaukee

Going to Molokai

You are standing huddled against your mother in a driving, hammering rain that has soaked you both to the skin. She has a tight hold on your hand, but she is not looking at you or speaking to you. She is staring through the curtain of rain out to sea, like everyone else in the sodden little group on the beach. They all have bundles, but they have long since given up trying to keep them dry. Yours lies at your feet, a roll of palm-leaf matting that holds everything you possess in the world. You are shivering, not only because you are cold but also because you are very, very frightened.

Only a week ago the government inspector came to your village with a doctor who examined you and all your family and spoke very seriously to your mother. She began to cry, and everyone in the house — your father, your sisters, your grandmother, and your uncle — tried to explain to the doctor that the yellow marks on your arms and the lump on your ear were nothing bad. But he took no notice of them and wrote your name and your mother's name on a piece of printed paper.

After that it was all muddle and crying, until now, here you both are, waiting on the stony beach for the boat that is to take you to the island of Molokai, to the leper settlement on the isolated peninsula — the place you have heard called Makandu, which means "the given grave."

Your father has come with you, but only to say goodbye. He is fit and well, and though you had

ALL LEPERS ARE REQUIRED TO REPORT THEMSELVES TO THE GOVERNMENT HEALTH AUTHORITIES WITHIN FOURTEEN DAYS FROM THIS DATE FOR INSPECTION AND FINAL BANISHMENT TO MOLOKAI.

Local notice at the time, in Hawaii

A coasting schooner, of the kind the leprosy victims would have sailed in, moored off an Hawaiian island.

heard him trying to persuade your mother to let him go with you both, you know that he cannot come. There are too many people who need him at home.

Other people from your village have been sent to the lonely peninsula on Molokai. Your mother has told you that there will be friends waiting when you land, but all you can think of are the stories you have heard — that no one comes back from Makandu. You look at the other people on the beach, some with missing fingers or open wounds. You know that you will become as ill as they are. And you know that once aboard the boat you will never see your family or friends again.

Now a sigh murmurs through the waiting people. You look beyond them and see the boat. It is coming steadily closer. It looms out of the rain like a shadowy sea monster. A wail starts up all along the beach, and people cling to each other while the armed police, who have stood at some distance, move closer, guns ready.

It is time to go.

How it was

That child's experience is a terrible thing even to imagine, but about a hundred years ago, it happened to many, many people. Today, that same beach is busy with happy tourists, and Molokai is just another Hawaiian island where people go to enjoy the sun and scenery. The once-feared "leper" colony is simply a place for those tourists to visit. Leprosy itself has another name — Hansen's Disease — and it is now treated and cured.

People who have the illness are not called "lepers" any more. They are called "leprosy sufferers" or simply "people with leprosy." We now know that people who are ill with leprosy are just like you or me and that leprosy is just another curable disease. It is not even very catching.

But when people like the little child and its mother were sent to Molokai, there was no treatment and no cure. Everyone believed it to be the most fearsome and infectious disease in the world. Since biblical times, "leper" had meant something dark and dreadful to countless people.

Early sketches of leprosy sufferers. Top: patient, with physician. Bottom: with warning bell.

Neglected and untreated, it had a terrible effect on its victims, often making them hideously ugly and deformed. Healthy people were terrified of catching it, so they sent anyone suspected of having it as far away as possible. If you go into very old churches, you may see "squints," little slit windows that allowed the "lepers" to see the altar without entering the building.

No one knows how long the illness has existed. In the Middle Ages, the word "leper" filled everyone with terror. People who had leprosy had the funeral service said over them, just as if they were already dead. They were given a bell or a rattle to warn everyone to keep away and were sent off to live as

"And the leper in whom the plague is, his clothes shall be rent, and the hair of his head shall go loose, and he shall cover his upper lip and shall cry unclean, unclean."
Leviticus XIII, 45

7

*Above: Thirteenth
century engraving of a
"leper" with begging
bowl to warn he is
"unclean." During this
period leprosy was at its
worst: one in four
people in Europe had
leprosy. It thrived where
people were poor, badly
fed, and dirty.*

*Right: "Room for the
Leper! Room!" An
illustration by Nathaniel
Willis in the 1870s, when
Father Damien had just
started his work with the
leprosy sufferers on
Molokai.*

"Lepers" begging on the roadside in Morocco in 1887. They were confined to a village outside the city walls.

best they could. Some monasteries built places where they could find shelter, but most lived out a lonely and desperate life. It is especially sad to realize that many of them did not have leprosy at all, but only skin conditions that frightened other people.

Despite medical advances over the centuries, the old, old fear was still there. People sent to Molokai were still outcasts, and the same mistakes were still being made. It was a terrible place.

But just over one hundred years ago, one brave and good man was to help change life for everyone with leprosy, not only on Molokai but all over the world. His name was Damien.

Jef becomes Damien

Josef de Veuster-Wouters was born in Tremeloo in Belgium on January 3, 1840. He grew up a cheerful,

BELGIUM
One nation – three languages

Tremeloo
Brussels • Louvain
BELGIUM

NETHERLANDS
GERMANY

Multi-lingual

Flemish-speaking

French-speaking

German-speaking

Brussels
Tremeloo
Louvain
LUXEMBURG
FRANCE
Paris

Belgium became a separate kingdom only in 1830, which explains the different languages spoken in its various regions. It was previously divided between France and the Netherlands.

ordinary boy, known to everyone as Jef. He lived a happy life at home, often helping the local builder, Janneke Roef. He learned carpentry and did all kinds of odd jobs for him. Jef had no idea how much he was to need those skills in the years ahead.

His was a solid and respectable Flemish family. Two of his sisters had become nuns, and one brother had entered a religious order and was now called Father Pamphile. Jef's father wanted him to go into business and build a successful career for himself.

But businessmen had to know French, and in Jef's part of Belgium everyone spoke Flemish. So when he was in his teens, he was sent off to study in the French-speaking part of the country. At first, the local students mocked him for being a Flemish-speaking country boy, but Jef had a handy pair of fists and was able to defend himself. He was not exceptionally clever, but he was determined: by making a great effort, he became fluent in French in a surprisingly short time.

By the age of eighteen, Jef had made friends and was making good progress in his studies, but he felt restless and miserable. He was becoming increasingly more certain that he did not want to go into business. He would far rather be a priest. So he decided to join the Fathers of the Sacred Hearts or Picpus Fathers, as his brother Pamphile had done.

Now came the difficult part. He hated to disappoint his parents because he knew how they had had to struggle and save to send him to college. But when he told them what he wanted to do, they understood. They knew he had thought about being a priest for a long time, and all they wanted was for him to be happy.

So Jef went off to Louvain in 1859; he entered the Order and took the name of Damien. With no knowledge of Latin, he could not study for the priesthood as he had hoped, but he was accepted as an ordinary Lay Brother.

He was a fit, strong young man, and his carpentry and building experience soon came in handy. A new chapel was being built and a tall chimney stood in the way. It looked dangerous indeed, and none of the local workmen would touch it. Damien clambered up the ladder, and perched high above the flabbergasted onlookers, he got down to the job of dismantling it, brick by brick.

His determination did not stop at chimneys. He got Pamphile to teach him Latin in any spare moments they could find, and soon he'd made such progress that his superiors could not help but be impressed. After six months they allowed him to begin to study for the priesthood.

Long after, people were to say that Damien was an ignorant peasant, but that was never true. Although he was not a brilliant scholar, he already spoke two languages. Then in 1860 he was sent to Paris to learn Latin, Greek, and philosophy.

After that he went back to Louvain to study theology. He did not find all the work easy, but he very badly wanted to be a priest.

He also wanted to go out and work in the Pacific

Damien in 1863, when he was twenty-three years old. He was a brother with the Sacred Hearts Fathers but had not yet been ordained a priest.

islands. When Damien was twenty-one, a Bishop from Hawaii had given a talk to the students in Paris and had told them he would like to take some young priests back with him. Damien desperately wanted to go, but he was not yet a priest. To make it harder to bear, his brother was one of those chosen. Poor Damien's heart sank, but then came the chance that was to change his life as well as the lives of thousands of people.

There was an epidemic of a fever called typhus. Many people were dying, and when Pamphile caught it, Damien was terribly worried. Pamphile was very sick indeed, and though at last he began to get better, he was far too weak to make the long journey to the Pacific islands.

Damien saw his chance. He knew his superior would probably not let him go, so he wrote directly to the head of his Order, begging him to take him instead of Pamphile, even though he was not yet a priest. The Superior General must have liked this eager, determined — and rather disobedient —young man, because he agreed that he could go with him.

And so it was Damien, not Pamphile, who set sail in November 1863 on the four-month voyage around Cape Horn to the other side of the world, leaving behind all the old familiar things. He was sailing to a life unlike anything he had ever known.

The island that needed a friend

Turn the pages of the atlas until you find a map of the vast Pacific Ocean. Scattered across it lie chains of islands like bright beads, with beautiful, magical names. Héréhérétué, Aitutaki, Rarotonga, Arorae, Nukunonu, Kusaie, Nihoa, Oahu, Yap. The explorers who discovered them were bewitched by their beauty — the flowers, the dazzling fish that flickered among the reefs, and the happy, friendly people.

Tragically, the newcomers brought with them most unwelcome gifts: sicknesses like measles and the common cold. These meant little in Europe, but they killed thousands of the islanders.

Worst of all, the Chinese who came to work on

the islands unknowingly brought with them the most feared disease of all — leprosy. The Hawaiian people called it *Ma'i Pake*, the Chinese Disease.

A Hawaiian outrigger canoe of the sort in which Damien had his adventure.

By 1865, the government of the Hawaiian islands, which lie in the northern Pacific, had become so frightened by the spread of the illness that it decided that everyone who caught it must be sent to an isolated peninsula called Kalaupapa, on the north coast of the island of Molokai. That may seem a very cruel thing to do, but in those days no one knew much about leprosy. The only way to stop it from spreading seemed to be to keep leprosy sufferers away from healthy people.

What was wrong, however, was that no one seemed to bother about what happened to the sick people once they were on the island. The old saying, "Out of sight, out of mind," seemed to be true of Molokai Island.

The first people who landed at Kalaupapa were given a supply of seeds and tools. However, no one realized that because their hands and feet were rotting

An aerial view of the Kalaupapa peninsula on Molokai, where shiploads of people with leprosy were exiled. The cliffs formed an impassable barricade to the other side of the island.

Opposite: The Hawaiian group consists of over twenty volcanic islands and atolls. Here are the six main islands, including Molokai, which is only ten miles across from north to south. On the north coast, the map shows a bump, which is the peninsula where the leprosy colony was.

away or twisted and nearly useless, it was quite impossible for them to use the equipment.

The huts they were to live in had been hastily thrown together and were made from branches, leaves, and grass. A building called "the hospital" had been put up, but as there were no beds in it, no medicines, and no doctor, it could scarcely be thought of as one.

People died not from the disease but from starvation. They grew so desperate that they ran wild — fighting, drinking, and gambling. The government sent troops to try to restore order, but they were too afraid of catching leprosy to go anywhere near the offenders.

To try to pacify them, the government sent out a few cattle, some clothes and food, and a man to take charge. He stayed for only a few weeks and then went back to Honolulu, leaving the people convinced that no one cared at all what happened to them.

Everyone on the other islands knew what it was like there. Even the name "Molokai" made them afraid! The sick people, who were wrenched away

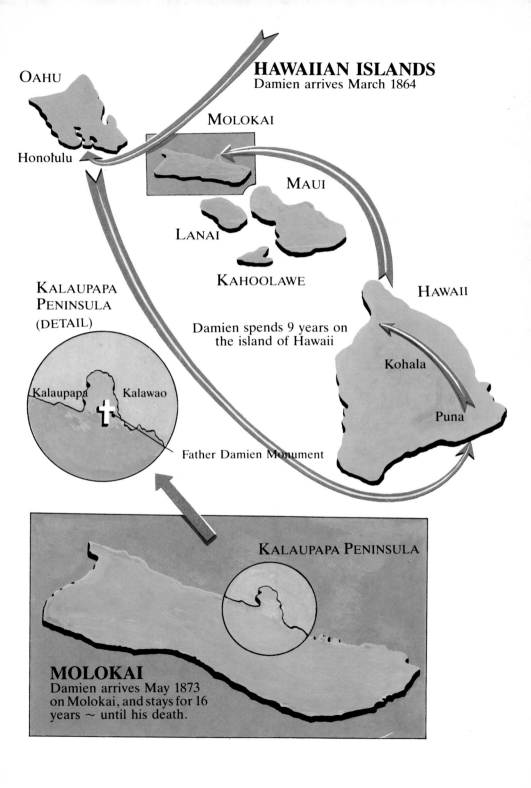

HAWAIIAN ISLANDS
Damien arrives March 1864

OAHU

Honolulu

MOLOKAI

MAUI

LANAI

KAHOOLAWE

HAWAII

Damien spends 9 years on
the island of Hawaii

Kohala

Puna

KALAUPAPA
PENINSULA
(DETAIL)

Kalaupapa   Kalawao

Father Damien Monument

KALAUPAPA PENINSULA

MOLOKAI
Damien arrives May 1873
on Molokai, and stays for 16
years ~ until his death.

from their homes and families and friends, were sometimes so mad with grief and despair that they fought not to be unloaded into the rowing boats that ferried them from the ship to the landing stage at Kalaupapa. If they did fight, they were thrown overboard to struggle to shore as best they could or to drown. Those who were landed by boat often had their few belongings stolen almost at once. They found themselves in a world where there seemed no hope at all. They were told "*Aole kanawai ma keia wahi* " — "In this place, there is no law."

You can imagine how the child and its mother must have felt when they were bundled onto the beach and led away over the rough road to Kalawao, with its filthy windowless huts and its population of desperately sick people, knowing there was never to be any escape.

They did not know that on the other side of the world, Damien was setting sail. He would eventually come to the island to be their friend and helper.

Hawaii at last

If you were told that you were going to the Hawaiian islands, I expect you would be very excited. You could find out a great deal about them from television, books, and glossy photographs, and you would know that they were only a few hours away by plane from your home.

In 1863, when Damien set out with other young men and dedicated nuns, it was nothing like that. Damien was excited, even though all he knew about his new home he'd learned from people and from books. It seemed to be an immense distance away, and the journey took four months by sailing ship. The vessel arrived in March 1864, when Damien was twenty-four.

They were to land at Honolulu, on Oahu. Even then it was a fine city, with a busy port and grand buildings. But the islands had not been altered as much as they have today.

Can you imagine what it must have been like — those first glimpses of the islands rising from the

glittering sea, the scent of flowers, and leaves drifting across the water? The passengers must have crowded to the ship's rail to watch the coast become clearer. Perhaps, as they followed the shore line, they saw canoes come out to greet them and brown-skinned children swimming like fish in the clear water.

Coconut palms, just one of the many new plants and trees Damien would have encountered.

The nuns and young men who went to serve on the island were welcomed by the missionaries and soon settled in. Damien at once started to learn what was by now his *fifth* language, Kanaka, so that he could speak to the local people in their own tongue. He also completed the studies he had kept up on the journey out. Two months after arriving, he was ordained a priest and, a little nervous of course, was sent off to his very first job, a run-down Mission in Puna, on Hawaii Island.

Nine years on Hawaii Island

When Damien arrived, the people were friendly and welcoming, but Damien found it quite unlike the life he had lived in Europe. In those days before television, people from the West were puzzled and

bewildered by those who lived a life so different from their own.

Still, he built a house and a church and began his work, calling people to mass not by ringing a bell but by blowing on a conch shell. The people were kind, but he missed his friends. He was sometimes so lonely that he would trek for miles across difficult country just for a few hours conversation with another priest. This loneliness was to haunt him all his life.

In March 1865, he heard that Father Clemens, whom he had met on the ship, was exhausted because his Mission in Kohala covered two thousand square miles. Damien suggested they trade places. Once there, he heard of an even more remote area near his Mission where there were some Christians. He set off by canoe to visit them. It capsized in heavy seas; he and the crew survived only by hanging on to the upturned boat and dog paddling to shore. He was shaken by the experience, but when he wrote home, he was careful to make it sound like an amusing adventure. Damien always kept his letters to his family cheerful, telling the whole truth to only his brother Pamphile.

As you will have guessed, such a near-catastrophe was not going to deter Damien. He set off again, this time by the dangerous overland route that he had tried to avoid. He rode as far as he could, but when the path got too bad, he was forced to dismount and struggle the rest of the way on foot. This trip took him four days.

This new area needed a church, so with the help of the local people, Damien set to work. He used the skills he had learned as a boy, and the building soon took shape. Everyone was astounded by his strength and skill, as he manhandled the biggest timbers into

"You could not wish for better people; gentle, pleasant-mannered, exceedingly tender-hearted, they neither seek to amass riches, or live in luxury, or dress much, but are most hospitable, and ready to deprive themselves even of necessities in order to supply your every want if you have to ask a night's shelter from them."
Father Damien, in a letter
to his brother,
FatherPamphile, dated
August 8, 1864

19

place and scrambled about on the roof. They all felt they had to work harder to keep up with him. It was a hard life, but Damien had learned he was happiest when he was busy.

He was learning more about the islands every day. You have probably seen earthquakes and volcanoes on television. Although they look wonderfully dramatic and exciting, Damien did not find them so. Two weeks of earthquakes caused great devastation in the countryside and villages, and forty of his newfound friends were killed. Later in his life, when visitors talked to him about the magnificence of volcanic eruptions, he could never share their enthusiasm.

Goodbye to Kohala

The little villages were widely scattered, which meant long journeys in all kinds of weather. Hawaii is one of the most beautiful places in the world, but it probably did not seem so when Damien was pushing his way through undergrowth in slashing rain.

The forests of tree ferns were full of beautiful flowers, and the dramatic beaches were dotted with the twisted shapes of crumbling black lava. But Damien had little time to consider their beauty. Instead, he was thankful indeed when, in October 1869, a young priest named Father Aubert was sent to help him.

Damien scarcely gave him time to get his breath back after his journey before setting him to work. Damien could never see why others could not work as hard or as long as he himself was able to!

The two men liked each other, but they scarcely ever saw one another, as they had to work so many miles apart most of the time. They were always busy. Life was interesting and went along without too many problems for nearly nine years.

Then in May 1873 Damein and Father Aubert were asked to take part in the celebrations at the consecration of a new church at Wailuku, on Maui. While they were there, Bishop Maigret spoke about the terrible conditions on Molokai and also about the

"So far, my children, you have been left alone and uncared for. But you shall be so no longer. Behold, I have brought you one who will be a father to you, and who loves you so much that for your welfare, and for the sake of your immortal souls, he does not hesitate to become one of you, to live and die with you."

Bishop Maigret, in a speech to the leprosy sufferers of Molokai on Damien's arrival, May 11, 1873

people there who had begged him to send a priest to be their friend.

Damien had seen new victims of leprosy rounded up and bullied aboard the ships bound for Molokai. He could not forget the look of terror and despair on their faces. When the Bishop asked for volunteers, he and three other priests all offered to go at once.

Bishop Maigret was deeply moved. He said he would never send people to such a dreadful place unless they were willing to go, and he was grateful to them. His idea was that they should take turns on the island, and he decided that Damien, fit and strong and capable, should be the first.

The Bishop was leaving to go back to Honolulu almost immediately, and his boat, the *Kilauea*, was going to call at the leprosy peninsula on Molokai on the way. They were going to land a cargo of cattle and a group of fifty leprosy sufferers. Damien could go with them.

Hastily, Damien said goodbye to his friends and went aboard, his head spinning a little at the sudden

Volcanic eruptions are common on the Hawaiian islands. They are dramatic and beautiful, but they can cause much suffering for the local people.

21

change in his life. He thought that he would take a look around the settlement and see what needed to be done, never dreaming that he would never see Kohala again. He was then thirty-three years old.

The world of Molokai

At last the ship dropped anchor off the unfamiliar shore near Kalaupapa village. Towering green cliffs, ribboned with waterfalls, plunged down to the boulder-strewn beaches. To the frightened passengers, they seemed like impassable prison walls, shutting them off from the rest of the island. They knew they would never again be allowed off the island. It was May 11, 1873.

Cargo and people were landed and Damien followed them, the Bishop going with him as far as the beach. Damien had seen leprosy before, but what he saw now horrified him. The people were dirty and disfigured. In many cases, the disease was far advanced, and their hands and feet were mere stumps. They looked less like men and women than terrible ghosts.

As the breakers roared up the beach behind them, Bishop Maigret spoke to the little crowd, telling them that Father Damien was the priest they had asked for, and that he would stay and look after them. Then he said goodbye to Damien. Dropping his voice, he told him to take great care, then turned and went back to the boat that was waiting for him in the surf.

As the ship moved away, Damien felt horror and loneliness sweep over him. His previous work had been hard, but he could see at a glance that these people would need far more help. He felt that he had neither the skills nor the knowledge needed for such a job. But he decided to tackle things a day at a time. After all, he was better than nothing!

His first sight of the leper village of Kalawao, at the foot of the cliffs, stunned him. It was far worse than anything he had imagined. As he looked around him, he realized that any idea of finding an abandoned hut to sleep in must be forgotten. Those he saw were windowless and dark. They were filthy

and stinking.

The islanders were not like the cheerful, friendly, laughing people he had left behind. Misery and fear had made them suspicious of strangers. They did not believe that he would stay, and they stared at him with blank eyes or with real anger. Damien knew that it would do no good to rush them. He must take things very quietly, letting them see that he really did want to help them.

A little chapel stood abandoned in the middle of the tangle of huts they called the village. Damien made himself a broom of palm leaves and began to sweep the floor. There were holes in the walls. Litter was scattered everywhere. Damien cleared away the debris and filled in the holes, quietly busy.

Gradually people came to watch, though no one offered to help. Damien noted that although many people were badly affected by the leprosy, some showed scarcely any marks of it at all. This new priest seemed to them a very ordinary sort of man, still young, rather good-looking, and not at all

The original landing beach on the Kalaupapa peninsula, Molokai.

bothered by their appearance. And kind — not at all like officials or inspectors.

A woman brought him some fruit on a leaf, and Damien took it from her. He smiled and thanked her in Kanaka. They stared. He spoke their language. He knew the correct forms of greeting!

Someone brought in a spray of flowers and put them on the altar. Damien heaved a hidden sigh of relief. It looked as though they would, after all, accept him as their friend.

He raised his eyes to the frighteningly disfigured group that stood near the door and resolved there and then that however terrible their appearance, he would never ever allow them to see any sign of revulsion on his face. They had enough to bear, and it would hurt them too deeply. Somehow he must hide his feelings and look through the ugliness to the person inside.

A waking nightmare

Damien found that one of the hardest things to bear as he explored the village was the appalling smell of the huts, the people, and the loathsome graveyard. Luckily, he had with him something that would solve the problem. From then on, he marched around the island puffing on his pipe, behind a cloud of overpoweringly strong-smelling tobacco.

At the end of the first day, he lay down to sleep under a pandanus tree, which was to be his bed until he had managed to build himself a little house. It had all happened so suddenly that it still did not seem quite real, but he was far too tired to stay awake thinking about it. He closed his eyes on stars and trees and village and went to sleep. The next morning when he woke, the nightmare was still there.

The more he explored the peninsula and the two villages, the more horrified he became. Everywhere was dirt and neglect. The people had lost all pride and any hope of things ever getting better. How could even the best of men and women fight the dirt when every drop of water had to be carried half a mile with crippled hands and feet? How could they look after their injuries when there were no medicines and no bandages?

The task ahead

In the eight years since the colony was first set up, scarcely a thing had been done to make their lives any better. No wonder they were suspicious of Damien. Many had given up any attempt to live a normal life. They passed their days and nights in drunkenness and gambling. Some terrorized the weak, stealing the little they had. And far worse, others took orphaned children to live as their slaves, abandoning them when they became too sick and weak to work for them any more.

"Here there is no law." Damien kept hearing those words as he went around the villages. They worried him far more than the poverty, sickness and dirt. What could he do? He was fit and strong, but he was alone. All he had was his strength, his common sense, his courage.

And his temper.

A temper seems an odd thing for a priest to need, but Damien knew that if he wanted to bring order, safety, and sanity to the settlement, he must use his

The ruins of an old leprosy settlement at Kalawao. There was no house for Damien, so he slept under a pandanus tree on his first night.

This African leprosy victim shows how leprosy can damage the hands and feet. Eventually people are unable to walk, dress, cook, or care for themselves. In Father Damien's time, the complications from infected wounds were horrible and led to death.

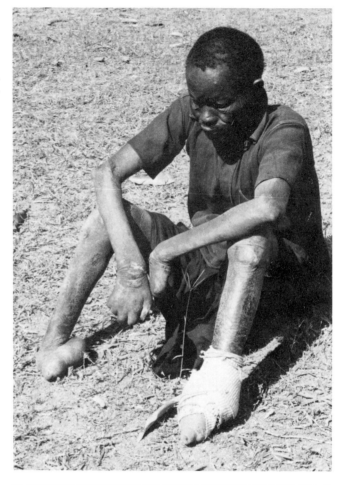

One of the main reasons for the fear and rejection of leprosy sufferers has always been that leprosy is one of the most disfiguring diseases in the world.

26

and act quickly. As he lay trying to sleep, he could hear the raucous laughter, the shrieking, and the shouting as the drunks staggered around the village. Kind words would do no good.

He leaped to his feet and chased the drunks. If the people of Molokai had expected a meek and mild priest who would allow them to go on in the same old way, they were mistaken. Damien roared out of the darkness, wielding his stick.

In the first weeks, he smashed the idols that they had used to frighten the ignorant and invaded the huts to rescue the orphaned children, ignoring the protests of their captors. The bullies cowered away from him, and little by little, Damien brought order back to Kalawao.

He was not only angry with the things that were wrong but was also worried about the non-Christian customs of the people who still followed their old traditions. He did not understand them, much less sympathize with them. It would be many years before white people realized how much they could learn from those they had regarded as "heathens" "savages," or "ignorant natives."

For all that, Damien wanted the settlers to have a far better life than the one they had. He believed they needed someone like him to help them regain their self-respect.

Beginnings

What could Damin do? There was so much that needed doing he scarcely knew where to start.

It is not likely nowadays that a priest would be left alone to cope with such difficulties. Even if he were, he would probably be given some basic medical training. He would arrive weighed down with medicines and sterile bandages, surgical instruments, disinfectants and, best of all, a radio to call for help or advice, or even a helicopter to fly in blankets or clothing or food supplies. Or a doctor. At any rate, he could speak to his friends.

Damien had nothing. There was no treatment and no cure. There was not even a clean piece of rag to

"Discolored patches appear on the skin, especially on the cheeks, and the parts affected lose their feeling. After a time, this discoloration covers the entire body; then ulcers begin to open, chiefly at the extremities. The flesh is eaten away and gives out a fetid odor; even the breath of the leper becomes so foul that the air around is poisoned with it. I have had great difficulty in getting accustomed to such an atmosphere."
Father Damien

"[In 1873] the huts were small, makeshift affairs of grass or branches or sugarcane leaves, with no ventilation. The wind often blew them to the ground or destroyed them entirely. . . . The many who had open sores on their feet, could not get about; and these and others in all stages of the putrescent disease lay about in the tiny fetid huts."
Charles J. Dutton, from The Samaritans of Molokai

The interior of St. Philomena, where Father Damien performed his religious duties as a priest.

"I found on my arrival [on Molokai] a little chapel dedicated to St. Philomena, but that was all. No house to shelter me. I lived for a long time under the shelter of a tree...."

Father Damien, in a letter to his brother, Father Pamphile, dated November 25, 1873

bandage up the sores and injuries.

But he still had his temper.

While he went about his new work, he began to bombard the government in Honolulu with letters — asking, pleading, demanding the basic things he needed. He needed *everything*. This was the start of his lifelong career as the man on Molokai who always wanted something and would nag and nag until he got it. Or so the officials felt. While he waited for answers, he did what he could with what was available.

There was no judge or policeman, no teacher, no doctor or nurse, no expert on building or farming or anything else on the peninsula. Damien had to be all these, on his own. He settled arguments, cleaned and bandaged wounds, repaired the hospital and the church, all in addition to his duties as a priest. These took up to two hours each day, and throughout all the crises Damien — *Father Damien* — never neglected the people he'd come to serve.

He had always worked twice as hard as everyone else. Now he worked even harder. He got some of the fitter men to clear little patches of land and plant sweet potatoes. That not only gave them something to do and to think about but added to their food supply. Their crops were so good that they were able to sell the surplus and make a little money to spend on things they needed. It made them feel they were normal human beings again.

Not everything was so cheerful. People died every day. He nursed them, held their hands, and comforted them, but he could not save their lives.

At least they did not die alone.

Funerals

The first funeral shocked him. The people of the village did their best to bury their friends with respect and love, but they could only scrape out shallow graves and wrap the dead in matting. Wild pigs invaded the graveyard, rooting out the bodies and scattering bones everywhere.

Damien resolved that everyone who died should at least have a decent burial. He made proper coffins and dug deep graves and said the funeral prayers. *In his first six years on Molokai, he was to make most of the coffins and dig graves for 1,600 people.*

But he knew that a tidy, peaceful graveyard, clean bandages, and better food were not enough. These people had lived lives without joy, grace, or music for so long that it was no wonder they turned to drink and despair. Damien went out of his way to make the church services as beautiful as he knew how. He sent to Honolulu for a bell and made the building bright with fresh flowers.

Few came to his church in the beginning, but gradually more and more ventured in to be together, to sing, and to hear what Damien had to say to them.

These idols are examples of Hawaiian art. The native people were happy, outgoing, and artistic. They worshipped their own gods. Father Damien worked hard to convert the people to Catholicism.

29

It helped them feel less cut off from the world beyond the sea and the Pali cliffs. Besides, his sermons started with the words "We lepers." No one else had ever said that before.

The first help arrives

The newspapers on Oahu and Hawaii soon heard about Damien and published articles about his work. People who read them felt guilty that they had never thought much about Molokai before. They began organizing collections of food and clothing for Damien and his people.

Some of the other church leaders were not at all pleased by the publicity. They thought the praise might go to Damien's head, but Damien was far too busy to think about newspapers. His only concern was the people under his care.

They knew him well now, and they wrote to Maigret asking if he could stay with them forever. The Bishop's reply was that nothing definite had been decided yet but that Damien could stay until further notice.

He stayed for sixteen years, until he died.

Days away

Damien was at first tied to the settlement. He went to Honolulu once, in July 1873, to collect all the good things people had collected for him — and to argue with the government for more help. Horrified, the government said he must never leave the peninsula again. He must not even board the boat that called there, to have a word with friends who were aboard.

"The average of deaths is about one a day. Many are so destitute that there is nothing to defray their burial expenses. They are simply wrapt in a blanket. As far as my duties allow me time, I make coffins myself for these people."

Father Damien, in a
letter to his brother,
Father Pamphile, dated
November 25, 1873

This was almost too much for Damien to bear. He could not believe it. He, a healthy man, was to be condemned to the life of a "leper" He had never been so hurt or depressed.

Then one night he had a surprise. His old friend, Father Aubert, who seems to have been a little like Damien himself, strode in from the darkness — in disguise! The two old friends talked and laughed the night away and when Aubert left at dawn, Damien felt far more cheerful. Aubert had told him that

The Palis of Molokai
have beautiful waterfalls
and many types of
flowers. The Hawaiian
islands lie in the Pacific
Ocean, thousands of
miles from both China to
the west and California to
the east. On the same
latitude as Hong Kong,
Hawaii is very hot. In
1898 Hawaii was
annexed by the United
States. On August 21,
1959, Hawaii became the
fiftieth state in the Union.

influential people were doing their very best to get the ban lifted, and after a very short time it was lifted, early in 1874.

Sometimes Damien longed to talk with someone outside the colony. When he did he would set off to climb the Pali cliffs, up the rough, dangerous track cut in 1874 that no person with advanced leprosy could manage. The cliffs were thick with undergrowth and dipped into deep, wet ravines. The going was hard, but Damien felt it was worth any struggle to visit his friend the superintendent on the "healthy" side of the island and travel about on the mule that was lent him. He never stayed away very long, for he knew his people needed him, but it lightened his heart and helped him to carry on with his lonely work.

He had long since given up any idea that he would ever be relieved of his job. He did not want to be, but he did wish that his superiors would send *someone* to help him — a doctor, another priest, or nuns to take care of the orphans, especially the little girls.

Peaceful days

Nearly ten months had passed and Damien had settled in as if he had never lived anywhere else. He had a little one-room hut now, with a thin mattress on the floor and some rather battered furniture. His clothes were growing shabbier with every passing week. His appearance might not worry people now, but in those days, many people who saw him were shocked. Priests were supposed to be clean and tidy people — a cut above ordinary mortal men — but Damien did *not* look very respectable or dignified.

In January 1874, Father André Burgermann had arrived on the "healthy" side of the island. One of his jobs was to build a new church there, but he had no idea how to go about it. So up over the Pali cliffs went Damien with his hammer. Father André looked after the settlement until Damien had organized and built the church. Then they changed places again.

It had been a break of sorts.

The bandaging of wounds and the funeral services

"He was always willing to leave off work for a time and join the children at their play. On almost any day he could be seen surrounded by romping, laughing youngsters playing tag with them or joining in other childish games. When he joked with the officials, his laugh was always loudest."
Charles J. Dutton, from The Samaritans of Molokai

went on, but so did the weddings and the christenings. Happier times had come to Kalawao.

Damien still worried about the children, especially the orphans. He begged the Bishop to send nuns to look after them, but nothing happened. He could not understand why he got so little help, but the Bishop had problems outside Molokai while the Molokai peninsula was now Damien's whole world.

He continued to write to Pamphile, and it is through these letters that we know so much about Damien's work and his deep religious faith.

One of his letters was published in the Order's magazine. Once again, the superiors and brothers in Hawaii were indignant! They thought it was a sign of vanity in Damien, who had actually had nothing to do with it. Poor Damien — shabby and tired and severely overworked — he did not seem very vain to his villagers.

Damien was a deeply religious man and extremely proud of what his Order was achieving in the Hawaiian Islands. Even though the Bishop refused his demands and some of his fellow

Damien slept under a pandanus tree (or screwpine) when he first came to Molokai. These trees have a peculiar root system that holds the trunk away from the ground as if on stilts. Often the roots of the tree form a large cave.

34

missionaries were jealous, he never doubted his mission. God had called him to minister to the leprosy victims of Molokai, even unto death, and he accepted that call courageously and steadfastly, despite all the problems he had to contend with. That, of course, didn't stop him from continually writing letters — complaining and asking for more for his people.

The fight against *Ma'i Pake*

Weeks turned to months. Damien had been on Molokai over a year. He had struggled on with native helpers, willing and kindly but untrained. A Mr. Williamson, a leprosy sufferer from Europe, also did what he could at the hospital.

Every morning after he had said Mass in his clean, flower-bright church, Damien went on his rounds, finding out how people were and cleaning up their injuries with patient, gentle fingers. Often he had to make an excuse to dash out into the air for a few moments. The huts were in a dreadful state! How could he allow these suffering people to go on living

"I lived a long time under the shelter of a tree, not wishing to sleep under the same roof as the lepers. I was able to build myself a hut sixteen feet long and ten wide, where I am now writing these lines. Well, I have been here six months, surrounded by lepers, and I have not caught the infection."
Father Damien

An etching done in 1889 showing Father Damien's house and church.

in such wretched conditions?

Damien cared little for comfort or dignity for himself. All he wanted was care for his people. That was hard for some priests to accept, as they were used to respect and to being treated as if they were very important. He could get edgy at times, too. His battle with the officials, safe and snug on the bigger islands, was making him tired and bitter. He kept up his barrage of letters to the Hawaiian government, begging them to send timber, nails, tools, anything he could use to put up proper housing. The Hawaiian government behaved as though it were stone deaf. Damien was reaching the boiling point. There they sat in their comfortable offices, safe from the wind and the rain, while his people rotted away in disgusting shacks. He was just about to start another spate of letters when his problem was taken care of.

The typhoon

A typhoon hit Molokai in late 1874. All night long it raged, the sea roaring and crashing against the rocks, the palm trees lashing in the fury of the wind. The people huddled together as the rotten thatch of their homes was ripped away by the gale. The ramshackle huts simply disintegrated. Morning found a wet and dejected population, but Damien was delighted. He wrote once more. This time even the officials could not say that it was an unnecessary request. Of course, they grumbled and quibbled, but eventually a ship anchored and a load of timber and nails was put ashore. There were, of course, no carpenters or builders, but Damien and the villagers had repaired the church and fenced the graveyard — what were a few huts?

Many of the villagers were too sick to help, and some too lazy, but Damien had eight willing helpers. This time the houses were real houses, well made and decent places to live in. Damien saw to it that they were raised a little off the ground so that they did not get sodden and rot. Damien and his crew built three hundred houses in the end, and now he, too, had a proper house of his own instead of a hut. It was bare

Father Damien 1888
the Leper.

EDWARD CLIFFORD
189?

37

and poor, but it was dry and clean and a place where people could find him if they needed him.

At first, Damien remembered what the Bishop had said and would not allow anyone with leprosy to come into his house. He did not want to catch the disease, not only for his own sake, but because he wanted to stay healthy enough to work and to help his people. Women without the disease cooked his meals and cleaned his house. He thought that was a sensible precaution.

But he eventually decided, "Every day I work with these people, touch them, clean their wounds, breathe the air they breathe. Every day I dig their graves and bury their dead. It's a bit silly to ban them from the house."

So the villagers who, like the healthy islanders, enjoyed a little company and conversation used to drop in on Damien and spend a while in his room. He winced a little when they tried his pipe but said not a word. He was as healthy and strong as ever.

Bright days and dark days

Dirt and thirst. They still had to be tackled. The water supply on the peninsula had always been a nightmare. Whatever Damien had achieved, he knew he could not begin to make a decent life for them unless he could provide a reliable supply of clean water. And without water, diseases spread and crops couldn't grow.

There was a source of good water, but it was too far away to be of much use — over half a mile from Kalawao. It needed to be piped to the village, so he wrote to the government officers and asked for pipes. Nothing happened.

Damien wrote again. And again. And again. The government officers were tired of letters from Damien. So, probably to stop the flood of letters, they got him his pipes and taps. Not that they sent any engineers or plumbers to help fit it all up. No engineer or plumber would have dared to go near the settlement, as they would not have been allowed to leave again!

How Damien must have blessed the name of Janneke Roef. Once again, his childhood experience back in Belgium was there to help him. It certainly seemed to have been of far more use to him than his Latin and Greek.

He got together the fittest, strongest men he could find, and they set out to lay the pipes all the way from the distant pool to the settlement. It was hard work, hacking and digging and dragging the pipes to where they were needed. It took months of work, but one glorious day the people gathered in the villages to see the taps turned on for the first time and a steady stream of clear, cold, bright water gush into their bowls. There would be no more struggling along the track to the foot of the Palis. It was another huge step forward for the colony. The pipeline was extended to Kalaupapa in 1888.

> *"To my utter amazement, I saw him on his new church where he was roofing, giving orders to masons, workers and carpenters. And yet he has the appearance of a real leper, his face puffed, his ears swollen, his eyes blood-shot, and his voice hoarse. But that doesn't discourage him. He is happy. He works as though he were not sick at all, and he'll stop only when he drops."*
>
> Father Cornelius, about Father Damien, 1888

Visitors and friends

Times were changing, even in Hawaii. Perhaps Bishop Maigret had more courage than most, or perhaps he had more sense. He and Father Albert Montitor arrived on a pastoral visit in June 1875.

Damien was as pleased as a small boy, showing them the changes he had made, the improvements, the houses, the church. The people of the two villages were delighted beyond belief. Someone had remembered them. Someone important had praised their work and their priest.

A Dr. Woods came next, the Chief Medical Officer of Brooklyn Hospital in the United States. Woods had been all over the world, and he told Damien this was by far the best settlement he had ever seen. Damien positively glowed. His people were as pleased as he was. At last they had something to be proud of. He was still strong and handsome, but he told the doctor that he was quite sure he would become a leprosy sufferer in the end. The risks were too great for it not to happen. Despite all this, he seemed unworried and cheerful and excited about new projects.

An aerial view of the church built by Damien at Kalaupapa. Most of the noninfected people on the peninsula lived in this village.

New worries

If the old anxiety had lifted, new worries were on the horizon. Damien's good friend, the superintendent, had retired, and to Damien's horror, he himself was given the job. He felt he didn't have the right experience and would make a terrible mess of it. He was right. He did.

Mercifully, they soon found someone else. Unfortunately, it turned out that they had made a bad mistake. Damien had got into a muddle, but at least he had *tried*. This man meant well, but he did not work hard enough or keep an eye on the people under him. They could not be depended on, and Damien was to have endless trouble with them.

It was not until 1878 that another priest was sent to help him in his immense task. Unfortunately, Damien had a very quick temper and quarreled with both this man and the priest who replaced him in 1882. Damien never lost his temper with the leprosy victims, but he often did with people who came to help. He just couldn't understand why all the members of his Order were not as enthusiastic and tireless as he was. Damien was difficult to get along with. He was argumentative, obstinate, and disorganized. Joseph Dutton, who was later to become his willing helper, described him as "vehement and excitable in regard to matters that did not seem to him right and he sometimes said and did things that he afterwards regretted."

When the second priest left in 1885, Bishop Koeckmann refused Damien a replacement because he believed that if Damien had been less quarrelsome, the other priests would never have left. Unfortunately, by 1885, Damien was also suffering from leprosy himself and couldn't manage as well as he had in the past.

Things look up

All the same, things really *were* getting better. One of the leprosy sufferers had become a valuable friend and helper, and a new doctor, Dr. Emerson, had arrived on the island too.

Damien took to building again, this time an orphanage for the boys. He had already built one for the little girls and installed a lady to act as cook, housekeeper, and mother to them. Now forty boys were safely housed, though it was years before he could get adequate staff to look after them. Damien even built a school, which grew as the years went by.

Building occupied a great part of his life. He cleaned out and repaired the abandoned hospital that had been put up long before he came to Molokai. He then opened it with some of the more healthy girls as nurses. The new doctor brought medicines that could ease the symptoms a little, even though they did not cure the disease.

In 1881 came great excitement. Princess-Regent Liliuokalani was coming on a visit! She was the sister of the King of the Hawaiian Islands, David Kalakaua. Imagine the preparations — painting, scrubbing, garland-making, and singing practice. Damien had by now organized a choir that led the processions on feast days and a band that played instruments given by the Bishop.

"Oh, no! We're well off here. The government watches over us, the Superintendent is good, and we like our pastor. He builds our houses himself, he gives us tea, biscuits, sugar, and anything. We wouldn't want to leave if it meant we would have to leave our Makua Kamiano [Father Damien]."
Leprosy settlement villager, 1884

*Father Damien,
surrounded by young
boys from the orphanage.
Sometimes children with
leprosy were sent to
Molokai without their
parents. Often the parents
died of leprosy, leaving
their infected children to
cope alone.*

At last the Princess arrived with her sister, the prime minister and all their entourage. She was completely overwhelmed by the greeting she received and by the sight that met her eyes. Among the crowd, she recognized people she had known when they were fit and well. It was all too much for her. The Princess burst into tears and the prime minister had to make the speech.

Damien showed her some of the work that had been done. She was so impressed that when she got home she sent many things the settlement needed. On top of that, she bestowed on Damien the Order of Knight Commander of the Royal Order of Kalakaua. It sounds very grand indeed, but Damien put it at the bottom of a box and forgot about it.

The newspapers had a field day — and some of the more important people in the Church growled a little more — but Damien didn't worry about that. He was wonderfully happy.

Unfortunately, Dr. Emerson was not working out. He charged too much for his services and also had difficult ways. Damien was grateful when he left and Dr. Fitch, a kind and cheerful man, took over. He and Damien became very good friends. Though he was not a Catholic, he agreed wholeheartedly with Damien that they needed nuns to come to the island to help with the women and children.

In those days, Catholics and Protestants often disagreed violently. But Damien was discovering that Protestants could be fine people, and Protestants who met Damien were discovering the same thing about Catholics.

The royal visit

The royal visit must have been a very great success,

An aerial view of the leprosy village at Kalawao. While he was on Molokai, Damien and his helpers built over three hundred homes for the leprosy victims. He also built a hospital for one thousand patients plus two orphanages.

SOUVENIR.

ALOHA OE

(My love to you.)

MARCH.

The Queen Kapiolani. The Princess Liliuokalani.

Composed and arranged by

J. THOMAS BALDWIN.

Incorporating the popular Song "Aloha Oe"

BY THE

Princess Liliuokalani

And performed by

BALDWIN'S BOSTON CADET BAND

AT THE

Grand Reception given by the City of Boston to

Queen Kapiolani and Princess Liliuokalani

May 12th 1887.

for the Princess-Regent came back, and this time she brought Queen Kapiolani. The outcasts told them about all that still needed to be done. The clothing money sent by the government was inadequate: it would buy only one shirt and one blanket for each person. The food was often rotten when it landed. And even though the hospital had been opened, the coffin and the patient often went in the same cart!

Damien showed the Queen around. Because of bad food and water, enteritis was rife. The Queen was concerned about all these problems. She asked Damien searching questions and saw to it that many things he needed were sent at once. But she and others who saw the celebrations were dumbfounded by the joy and enthusiasm of the people, particularly the joy of the singers and musicians — despite their crippled hands and their disfigured faces.

Dark days

In 1883, a short time after he had told the doctor how fit he was, Damien discovered that his feet were painful and hot and that small yellow spots had appeared on his back. He guessed what it meant but said nothing.

There were more good things happening. Damien loved visitors, and now more people were coming to the island to see him. As they talked to him, they tried to find out more about the way he felt about his life, but he would not speak about himself. He would speak only about his "children," the people with leprosy. He kept his secret.

In time, the symptoms of leprosy faded but that turned out to be an illusion. One evening in 1885, as he was soaking his feet in a bowl of warm water to ease their aching, he realized that it was not warm at all but boiling. He had felt nothing.

Two settlement doctors, Dr. Arning and Dr. Mouritz, confirmed what he already knew — leprosy had caught up with him at last.

He told Pamphile in 1885, but in a letter to his mother, he just said he had scalded his feet rather badly but was almost well again.

Opposite: A music cover showing Queen Kapiolani and Princess Liliuokalani, who composed the song "Aloha Oe."

"I desire to express to you my admiration for the heroic and disinterested service you are rendering to the most unhappy of my servants; and to pay, in some measure, a public tribute to the devotion, patience and unbounded charity, with which you give yourself to the corporal and spiritual relief of these unfortunate people, who are necessarily deprived of the affectionate care of their relations and friends."

Princess-Regent Liliuokalani, in a letter to Father Damien, dated 1881

He heard that a Japanese doctor had, in 1886, evolved a new treatment to lessen the pain and slow down the progress of the disease. He wanted to try it, but the Father Provincial wrote a letter that hurt him bitterly. It said that if he came to Honolulu, he was to be shut in one room, for if people knew there was a "leper" in the Mission, they would keep away. If he chose to go to Kakaako, the hospital for suspected cases, he would not be allowed to celebrate Mass — the most important thing in a priest's life — because none of the other priests would use the Communion chalice and the vestments that he had used. Nor could he give Communion to anyone.

The letter ended by telling him that his wanting to go to Honolulu at all "shows us that you have neither delicate feeling, nor charity for your friends and that you think only of yourself."

This, to a man whose whole life was one of charity to his friends, the leprosy sufferers of Molokai, and whose only thoughts were of them. What could be more cruel?

Damien wrote back, saying that the letter had hurt him more than anything since his childhood. They were treating him as they treated his friends, the other sufferers from the disease, as if the sickness was evil and bad and made its victims so.

His right leg was now as bad as his left, and Dr. Mouritz said he simply must go to the hospital at Honolulu to try the new experiment.

The Sisters were determined to make his stay happy. Sister Antonella whitewashed a room and all the nuns donated their treasures — pictures and quilts and little statues — to make it as welcoming as they could.

It was all they could do to hide their tears when they saw how desperately ill he was. But for the first time in years, he slept between clean, white sheets and had nourishing meals cooked for him.

He was a terrible patient, escaping from his room to comfort patients waiting to be sent to Kalawao, reassuring them by telling them about the welcome they would have. The Sisters forgave him!

47

Unfortunately, the new treatment had no effect, and he soon had to say goodbye. He returned, for the last time, to Molokai.

Help arrives — Joseph Dutton

When he got home, there was a letter waiting for him. Pamphile, who was sick himself with tuberculosis, wanted to come to Hawaii to see him. Damien's Bishop was delighted and said Pamphile would be made very welcome, but the authorities in Belgium said he could not be spared.

They never saw one another again.

From Pamphile's next letter, he learned that their 83-year-old mother had died. Damien seemed to be at the very bottom of his life. He needed something wonderful to happen.

And it did.

In July 1886, Joseph Dutton arrived. An American born in 1843, he had fought in the Civil War and done different jobs in the States. His marriage had failed and he had decided, like Damien long before, to become a Trappist monk; but he was not happy in the life. Then one day, he read an article about Damien and the leprosy villages on Molokai.

Joseph packed his bags, took a ship, and suddenly turned up at Kalawao, telling the astounded Damien that he was going to stay with him and lend a hand as long as he was needed. He stayed over forty years, until he died. He was a man who could almost outwork Damien, strong and kind, with a sense of fun. He was the sort of man Damien had needed beside him all along, as friend and fellow worker all his time on the islands.

Damien asked if a new priest who had arrived in Honolulu could be sent out to him. The reply: "Father Sylvester does not feel that it is his vocation to bury himself with the 'lepers.' He does not even consider that it would be bearable to live among the healthy Hawaiians on the other side of the Palis, on account of the isolation and loneliness. A young missionary should not be discouraged."

Damien could hardly believe his eyes.

"I picture him as always ready to take up with great vigour anything that presented itself as his actual duty, and, further, anything at all that he thought would be good, whether it was actually his duty or not. Anything that appeared to him to be good — good to do — was something for immediate action; he apparently considered it really his duty. He did not give much time to the study of expediency, or the cost, or the danger."

Brother Joseph Dutton, on Father Damien, from The Samaritans of Molokai

More help — Mr. Chapman

In 1887, amidst the continuing worries, an unexpected letter came from a Church of England vicar in London, a Mr. Chapman. He praised Damien's work, offered his friendship — the thing Damien needed more than anything — and said he was collecting money to send out to him. He would like to have come himself, but he was too poor and too many people depended on him in London.

Damien was grateful. The man had scarcely anything himself, yet he could find money for a stranger half the world away. Damien had been brought up to be wary of Protestants, yet here was another who was goodness and kindness itself.

When the money arrived, it was double what he had promised. Damien was ecstatic! He would be able to buy good, serviceable clothing for all who

Aerial view of Kalaupapa village showing the church and landing stage. People still live in this village today, although Kalawao has been abandoned.

needed them. His joy was short-lived. His Father Provincial reprimanded him for spending the money without consulting anyone. Of course, Damien should have, but to Damien his people were far more important than rules and regulations. He often made mistakes, especially with money, but was always willing to learn. If someone pointed out, quietly and sensibly, where he had gone wrong, he would always see sense — and apologize.

Damien was growing more ill. He was hungry but felt awful the moment he ate anything. His heart was failing, his eyes growing dim, his voice fading to a whisper. His skin was horribly ulcerated and his nose damaged. The doctors were appalled to see how quickly leprosy moved through him. His ears were swollen, his eyebrows falling out, his left leg very painful. Still he forced himself to go on working.

Long after, people who knew him wrote that although he had been kind to the villagers before, now that he too had the disease, he became lighthearted. He played with the children and laughed and joked with the older people. It was as if he now felt he was one of them, a relative rather than their priest.

Damien had been a priest for nearly twenty-five years. That should have been a great cause for celebration, but in his gloomier moments, he felt there was little to celebrate. Three new priests had come to Honolulu, but none were to be spared for the leprosy settlement. He tried very hard not to be bitter, but he felt hurt.

More troubles — and Conrardy

The Franciscan Sisters he longed to have working on Molokai now wrote to Damien. They wanted to come but had been told that they would not be allowed to receive Communion from the hands of a "leper" and must wait until a healthy priest was living on the island.

In 1888, just as Damien began to feel like giving up, a priest called Lambert Conrardy arrived in

"I feel no repugnance when I hear the confessions of those near their end, whose wounds are full of maggots. Often, also, I scarce know how to administer Extreme Unction, when both hands and feet are nothing but raw wounds. This may give you some idea of my daily work. Picture to yourself a collection of huts with eight hundred lepers. No doctor. In fact, as there is no cure, there seems no place for a doctor's skill."

Father Damien

Honolulu, asking to be sent to help on Molokai.

Conrardy was eager to help, but he found it all far harder than he had anticipated. He could hardly bear to eat his food, fearing that it might have been touched by someone infected.

Perhaps Damien did not think, or perhaps he was quietly teasing him when he passed him a plate and assured him that *this*, at any rate, had not been touched by "a leper."

Conrardy was afraid, but he tried his best not to show it. One morning a dying child lurched out of a doorway and fell at his feet. Conrardy nearly fled. Damien gathered the little boy into his arms and comforted him, saying to Conrardy, "Thank heavens we got here when we did." Poor Conrardy felt ashamed and helped Damien, even though he could scarcely bear to touch the child. He was not yet like Damien. Damien could see the person beneath the illness, rather than the illness.

On the way back to the house, Damien told him that he had seen three consecutive colonies come and go since he had been on the island. Conrardy shuddered — and wondered how long he himself would last. But he stayed and was one of the priests still with Damien when he died.

The Sisters arrive

Damien had had leprosy for four years, but he had what is called a "remission," which is when a disease stops getting worse for a while. Now there were a thousand people in Kalawao, so Damien had to go on building. The latest project was a home for the girls, built with money from a Protestant banker.

Then, at long, long last, in November 1888 — the Franciscan Sisters arrived! Damien was so happy he forgot all his difficulties and disappointments. The little girls were in safe hands and would get some education too. He was feeling better — he had friends and he had good helpers.

Outsiders were astonished by his cheerfulness and the cheerfulness of everyone in the settlement. The

"Every morning then, after my Mass, which is followed by an instruction, I go to visit the sick, half of whom are Catholics. On entering each hut, I begin by offering to hear their confession. Those who refuse this spiritual help are not, therefore, refused temporal assistance, which is given to all without distinction."

Father Damien

frightened and dejected people who saw Damien arrive so long ago would scarcely have recognized the place. It was as though his own good, strong heart had brought life to the whole community.

Visitors who knew how ill he was (and expected to find him in bed) got a surprise. They were far more likely to find him astride the rooftop of his new church, giving instructions. He had given a lot of thought and love to its design. It was specially planned for his people.

When the church was finished, the Sisters were invited to see it and were quite startled. It was painted brightly, with riotous decorations. It was not at all like the bare white chapels they were accustomed to. It made them smile, but Damien's people thought it was beautiful.

He had come a long way since he felt worried and uneasy with the Hawaiian people. He had become part Hawaiian himself.

He had built a guest house so that visitors could live and sleep in a place untainted by leprosy. He would not go in, but sat outside when he went to talk with those who visited.

A cheerful, young Irish-Australian, Brother James, arrived to add to the growing number of friends and helpers he had about him. There were never enough, but the days were less lonely.

At Christmas, the Sisters gave Damien a pipe — a splendid Meerschaum pipe that delighted him. They would sometimes walk down to his house to visit him, but they had been told that they must never eat with him. One day he was so eager to give them a cup of coffee that they simply could not refuse. When they got home, they got a scolding from the Mother Superior, but soon there was a dismal figure at the door. It was Damien. He'd come to apologize for getting them into trouble.

An end and a beginning

Although Damien had been ill again, he refused to go to bed. It worried his friends terribly, for at times

"[Father Damien] is now forty-nine years old — a thick-set, strongly-built man with black curly hair and short beard, turning gray. His countenance must have been handsome, with a full, well-curved mouth and a short, straight nose; but he is now a good deal disfigured by leprosy, though not so badly as to make it anything but a pleasure to look at his bright, sensible face. His forehead is swollen and ridged, the eyebrows are gone, the nose somewhat sunk, and the ears are greatly enlarged."

Edward Clifford, from
Father Damien

they just could not see how he stayed on his feet. In the end, he had to have himself taken around in a little cart, but he still gave advice and encouragement in the whisper of a voice that was all that was left to him, glad to see his friends and the progress that was being made. As leprosy destroyed his body, he seemed to become even more cheerful and outgoing than he'd been all along — but he could not fight it off much longer.

At long last he was forced to take to his bed, the old mattress on the floor. He did not seem sad and certainly not afraid. His friends were around him, and though he still spoke about there being so much to do, he felt great joy in thinking about what had already been done.

He had seen death so often in his long years on Molokai that it was no stranger when it approached.

"Look at my hands," he said, as he if he were speaking of those of one of his patients. "All the wounds are healing and the crust is turning black. That's the sign of death."

He died on April 15, 1889, at just forty-nine. His

Father Damien, photographed in March 1889 when he was seriously ill. He had struggled to the altar every day as long as he had any strength.

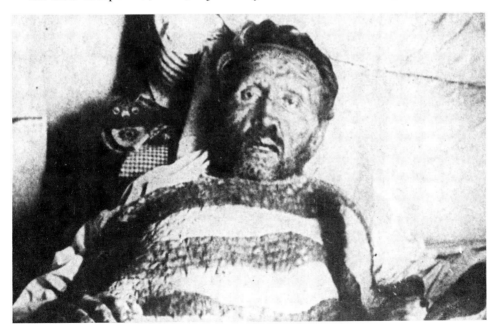

death was quiet and gentle, as if he were simply tired and glad at last to sink into a long, peaceful sleep. They buried him under the pandanus tree where he had slept that first night, when he had had his years of struggle stilll before him.

Damien, that difficult, kind, good man, was dead. But all over the world people who read about him and what he had done thought far harder than they had about the scourge of leprosy. Those who were working to find a cure and those nursing people already infected with the disease remembered him and gained courage.

Attack and Defense

There was one more ugly thing. The Rev. C. McE. Hyde, a minister living in Honolulu, sent a cruel letter about Damien to the Rev. H. B. Gage in Sydney, Australia, who then published it in *The Presbyterian*. It contained the remark, "The simple truth is, he was a coarse, dirty man, headstrong and bigoted" and worse.

It was a strange letter. Only four years before, Hyde had written of Damien as "this noble-hearted Catholic priest who went to Molokai in 1873 to care for the spiritual welfare of those of his faith and whose work has been so successful." Perhaps, for Hyde, who lived in great wealth and comfort in Hawaii, Damien had seemed *too* successful.

But good came of it, as it so often had come from the saddest things in Damien's life. Robert Louis Stevenson, the famous poet and author of *Treasure Island,* read the letter and was so appalled and angry that he wrote a long letter to the press, taking every point the minister had made and destroying it.

Dirty? "He was . . . but the clean Dr. Hyde was at his food in his fine house."

Headstrong? "Damien was headstrong. I believe you are right again; and I thank God for his strong head and heart."

It was a wonderful letter, and for Damien's friends, it made up a good deal for the lack of understanding that Damien had had to endure.

54

Some of those who spoke against Damien had said, "He had fallen into something of the ways and habits of a Kanaka," as if that were something terrible. It was one of the best things that Damien did. He lived like the people, ate like them, and claimed no privileges because he was white and educated and a priest.

No wonder the people who wanted to look important loathed him. In the cool, clean, white clothes they could afford, they thought to sneer at Damien's patched and shabby cassock. But all of them are forgotten now, while Damien is as loved and respected as when he died.

Only a few leprosy sufferers remain on the peninsula, and few can remember the days before the wonder drugs came. The little church of St. Philomena on Molokai is a place for tourists to visit

Damien's death spurred a worldwide effort to help leprosy sufferers. This picture shows Damien's body receiving a state funeral in Belgium, 46 years after he died.

55

Above: A view of the leprosy village of Kalawao, from the top of the Palis of Molokai.

now. But something of the old Molokai lingers like a ghost in the air of the peninsula, as if all who lived and died there are begging visitors never to forget.

Opposite: The statue of Damien, by Mansol, outside the Parliament Building at Honolulu. There were many complaints when it was first installed because Damien was shown suffering from leprosy.

Facts and Figures: Leprosy Today

Leprosy is still a major problem in many parts of Africa, South America and Asia, and one of the reasons for this is the same today as it was in Damien's day — fear.

When Damien was alive, the fear was understandable. There was no known cure, and the effects of leprosy were, as they still are, horrifying. There are two main forms of the disease — tuberculoid and lepromatous. The disease takes a different course depending on

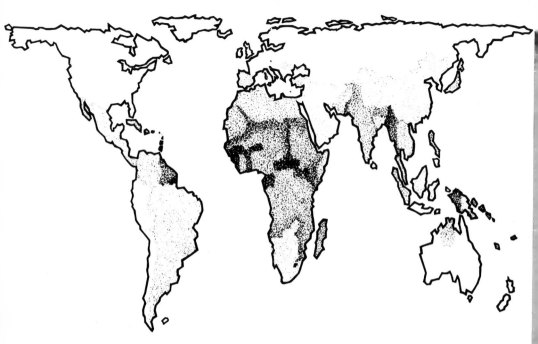

Now leprosy occurs mainly in the poorest countries, where living conditions make both discovery and treatment difficult. This computer simulation by LEPRA shows the number and location of victims worldwide — more dots show more sufferers.

which form the patient has. The body reacts vigorously to the tuberculoid germ or bacillus, causing irritation and whitish patches on the skin. Sometimes this form of the disease is mild and even cures itself. About seventy-five percent of leprosy sufferers have this sort of leprosy. But with the lepromatous bacillus, which is more infectious, the body doesn't seem to put up much of a fight, so very often no symptoms appear to begin with, even though the germs are multiplying rapidly. This means that the patient can be walking around possibly infecting others and by the time it is diagnosed, the disease has a serious grip on the body.

Whatever form is present, two main kinds of symptoms eventually emerge, affecting the skin and the nerves. The skin develops white patches and then large, lumpy nodules appear. At the same time, the bacillus attacks the nervous system, and the victim loses all feeling in some parts of the body. If patients cut their hands or scald their fingers or if they develop sores, they

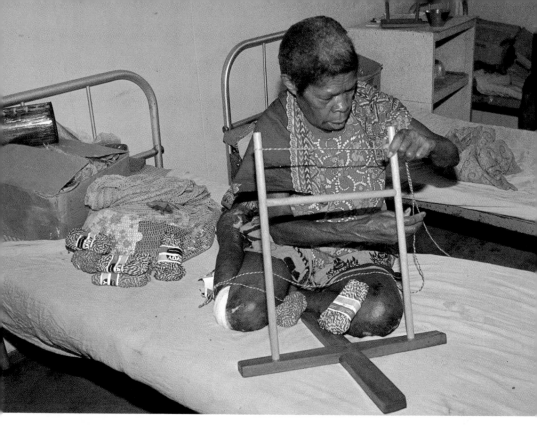

If leprosy is not treated, the sufferers lose fingers and toes. Often leprosy victims need to be taught a new profession because they cannot do what they used to. Here an African is learning to weave mats.

problem was that the bacilli, like the modern virus that causes AIDS, lie dormant for years, lurking in the body and waiting for their moment to strike. To conquer the disease with Dapsone, patients need to be absolutely regular in taking their doses of the drug. Poor and illiterate people often do not understand this. They either do not know they have the disease, or they take the first pills and when the whitish skin patches on their bodies disappear, they think they are cured. So they stop taking the pills. They go back to their remote villages, and the bacilli, almost but not quite knocked out by the drug, start to fight back, and in doing so develop an immunity against further doses. So when the disease does break out again — as it almost inevitably does in these circumstances — physicians find it is far, far harder to treat.

Before: The patient has ulceration on the face and his open wounds are likely to become infected.

Below: The early symptoms of leprosy are often not noticed. At Luimali Leper Hospital, a doctor examines a child whose mother had leprosy.

Other people are ashamed when they get the disease. They try to hide the fact, and by the time they are forced to seek treatment, the deformities are too great to eradicate completely even with plastic surgery.

Recently, two stronger drugs have been added to the doctor's weapons. Clofazimine and Rifampicin, used in a multiple attack on the disease, are quickly curing victims. But this happens only where the doctors have strict control over the treatment.

Nobody knows, even now, exactly how you catch leprosy. We do know that it is not quickly or easily caught, but every year, even in wealthy western countries, a few people come down with leprosy, picked up from their travels in Africa and elsewhere. About 250-300 cases per year are reported in the States. Nearly ninety percent of these cases are immigrants who bring the bacilli with them. There are small pockets of leprosy sufferers in Italy, Greece, and Malta;

about 350 cases in Britain; 3,000 in Portugal; and 4,000 in Spain.

Of course, it is in the poorer countries that leprosy really flourishes. There are four million cases in India. At least fifteen million people have the disease worldwide. Although leprosy kills, because it is so slow acting and usually confined to the poor, it does not feature highly in medical priorities. In India, for instance, medical students have only the shortest briefing about the disease, despite the high incidence.

One expert says it's "like trying to play marbles in the mud. . . . In theory, yes, leprosy today could be containable, with very intensive programs of training and retraining of existing staff. The problem is neither money nor drugs, but the overall level of competence—the keeping of records, the screening, the organizations, the follow-ups — and the fear and ignorance that keep patients away.

After: This is the same young man, feeling cheerful and looking years younger.

Below: An operation to rearrange the tendons of four fingers to restore movement to the partially paralyzed hand of a cured leprosy patient.

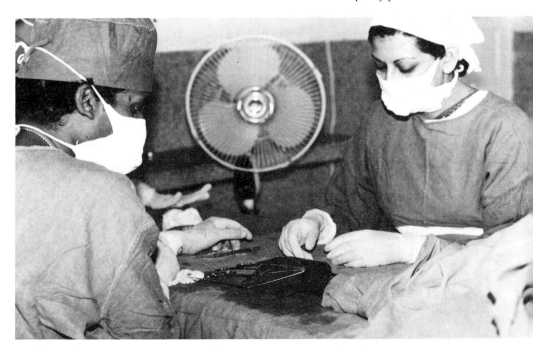

For More Information

Organizations

The organizations listed below can give you more information about Hansen's Disease (leprosy), about efforts being made to help people who suffer from the the disease, and about research being done on leprosy in the United States and in other countries. When you write to them, be sure to tell them exactly what you would like to know, and include your name, address, and age.

American Leprosy Mission
One Broadway
Elmwood Park, NJ 07407

U.S. Center for Disease Control
Building 1, Room 5045
1600 Clifton Road
Atlanta, GA 30333

Damien-Dutton Society for Leprosy Aid
616 Bedford Avenue
Bellmore, NY 11710

Gillis W. Long Hansen's Disease Center
Carville, LA 70721

World Health Authority
Avenue Appia
1211 Geneva 27
Switzerland

The Leprosy Mission
Suite 1128
67 Yonge Street
Toronto, Ontario
Canada M5E 1J8

Dehra Dun Leper Colony
The Center for Higher Consciousness
631 University Avenue NE
Minneapolis, MN 55413

Place to Visit

If you should go to Washington D.C., you might want to visit . . .

Statuary Hall, where in 1969, the state of Hawaii placed a statue of Father Damien, sculpted by Marisol Escobar.

Books

The following books will give you more information about Father Damien and the people he devoted his life to, and about the land he grew to love. Check your local library or bookstore to see if they have them or can order them for you.

About Father Damien —

Damien, the Leper Priest. Neimark (Morrow)

About Father Damien and other uncommon people —

Armed With Courage. McNeer and Ward (Abingdon)
Best Book of Heroes and Heroines. Evans (Doubleday)
Eleven Who Died. Hagedorn (Scholastic)
Heroes and Heroines of Many Lands. Strong (Hart)
Stories of Courage. Mackinnon (Franklin Watts)

About Hawaii —

Born in Fire: A Geological History of Hawaii. Rublowsky (Harper and Row)
Hawaii. Carpenter (Childrens Press)
Hawaii. Fergusson (Fideler)
Hawaii. Clark (Raintree)
Hawaii, the Aloha State. Bauer (Bess Press)
The Hawaiian Monarchy. Potter and Kasdon (Bess Press)
Hawaiians: An Island People. Pratt (Charles E. Tuttle)
Hawaiians of Old. Dunford (Bess Press)
Hawaii's Pathfinders. Rizzuto (Bess Press)

Glossary

Consecration
   A ceremony that makes something sacred so that it can be used for religious purposes. It was at the consecration of a church that Hawaii's Roman Catholic Bishop asked if one of his priests would volunteer to be sent to Molokai, and Father Damien agreed.

Missionary
   A person sent by a church to preach and teach about his or her religion, usually to a foreign land where the people don't have knowledge of the religion.

Monastery
   A place where people such as monks or nuns live isolated from the world. At one time, there were monasteries that provided for people suffering from leprosy.

Nodule
   A lump of tissue. A symptom of leprosy is the appearance of nodules on the body.

Peninsula
   An area of land that is almost completely surrounded by water, except at one point where it is connected to a larger body of land. On Molokai, the settlement for leprosy sufferers was on a peninsula that had water on three sides and cliffs on the fourth. The villagers were isolated because they could not climb those cliffs.

Priesthood

The vocation of a minister in a church. In the Roman Catholic Church, all priests are men and are called Father. Father Damien was a priest in the religious order called the Fathers of the Sacred Hearts.

Regent

A person who rules an area or acts in place of the ruler. Princess-Regent Liliuokalani was the regent for her brother, the King of the Hawaiian Islands.

Religious order

A group of priests, nuns, or brothers who live a certain way of life, usually a communal life. Some orders are known for their teaching, others for their quiet life of devotion to God. Others are missionaries.

Theology

The study of God and the universe, and of how man relates to them. In order to become a priest or nun, minister or rabbi, one must study theology for many years.

Typhoon

A violent cyclone or hurricane in the west Pacific. The storm can destroy just about everything in its path.

Chronology

1825 Pope Leo XII tells the Fathers of the Sacred Hearts that they will be in charge of Roman Catholic missions in the Hawaiian Islands. The first missionaries arrive two years later but are exiled by the government.

1840 **January 3** — Father Damien born Joseph de Veuster-Wouters, the seventh of eight children, in Tremeloo, Belgium.

1845 Joseph's sister Eugenia enters Ursuline Order.

1847 First search for a cure for leprosy begun by two Norwegian scientists.

1851 Eugenia dies of typhus.

1853 **August** — Joseph's brother Auguste enters a seminary, taking the religious name Pamphile.
Joseph's sister Pauline enters the Ursuline Order.

1859 **January** — Joseph enters Congregation of the Sacred Hearts of Jesus and

Mary and of Perpetual Adoration of the Most Blessed Sacrament of the Altar, also called the Fathers of the Sacred Hearts. He chooses Damien as his religious name and takes vows the next year.

1863   **October 30** — Damien sails from Bremerhaven, Germany, for Hawaii.

1864   **May 21** — Father Damien ordained a priest.
        July — Father Damien arrives at his mission in Puna district on Hawaii.

1865   **March** — Father Damien moves to Kohala parish on Hawaii. Leprosy settlement first established on a Kalaupapa peninsula on Molokai.

1873   **May 11** — Father Damien arrives on the Kalaupapa peninsula of Molokai.

1874   Dr. Karl Hansen of Norway discovers the bacteria that causes leprosy. Leprosy will eventually be called "Hansen's Disease" after Dr. Hansen.

1881   **September 8** — Father Albert Montiton comes to work with Father Damien. He stays until February 2, 1885.
        Princess—Regent Liliuokalani visits leprosy settlement and bestows Order of Kalakaua on Father Damien.

1883   Father Damien suspects that he has contracted leprosy.

1885   Father Damien's leprosy infection is confirmed by Dr. Arning.

1886   **July** — Joseph Dutton arrives.

1888   **May** — Father Conrardy joins Father Damien, as does Wendelin Moellers.
        November — Three Franciscan sisters arrive.

1889   **April 15** — Father Damien dies.

1908   Dapsone, a drug used to cure leprosy, discovered in Germany.

1936   Father Damien's body is returned to Belgium for a state funeral. His tomb is in the crypt of St. Joseph's chapel, Louvain, Belgium. Process begins in the Roman Catholic Church to make Father Damien a saint.

1948   Dapsone is first used extensively against leprosy.

1977   Father Damien is named "venerable" by Pope Paul VI, which is the last step before being officially recognized as a saint by the Roman Catholic Church.

Index